LETTERS FROM THE NORTH

Catholic Missionaries in Scandinavia
817-905 AD

Translated by: D.P. Curtin

Dalcassian
Publishing
Company
PHILADELPHIA, PA

LETTERS FROM THE NORTH

Copyright @ 2023 Dalcassian Publishing Company

All rights reserved. No part of this publication may be reproduced, distributed, or transmitted in any form or by any means, including photocopying, recording, or other electronic or mechanical methods, without the prior written permission of the publisher, except in the case of brief quotations embodied in critical reviews and certain other non-commercial uses permitted by copyright law. For permission request, write to Dalcassian Publishing Company at dalcassianpublishing at gmail.com

ISBN: 979-8-8692-7726-8 (Paperback)

Library of Congress Control Number:
Author: Curtin, D.P. (1985-)

Printed by Ingram Content Group, 1 Ingram Blvd, La Vergne, Tennessee

First printing edition 2023.

LETTERS FROM THE NORTH

The embassy of Ebbo, Archbishop of Reims, to the gentile Northern Nations, received by Pope Paschal.
(817 AD)

This was received by the Pope and strengthened by the privileges of the three succeeding Apostolics, namely, Paschal, Eugenius, or Gregory of the Holy See of Rome. To those who obstruct the terrible judgment of damnation, if the binding and loosing of the apostolic dignity can be the true testimony of God, who says: "Whatever you have bound on earth", and all the rest. Moreover, "what you did to one of the least of mine, you did to me"; as if he had offended one of the little ones; or else, the divinely promulgated tortures of the proud world. However, with pious and kind minds these things thus written down, they established by order of the inviolable apostolic laws.

The Pope's Easter letter to all Christians faithful to God

Paschal Bishop, the servant of the servants of God, to all the most holy brothers, co-bishops, priests, or other ecclesiastical orders, and to the most glorious Princes, Dukes, or magnificent Counts, and to all God's faithful Christians. Since it is most religious to exercise care and concern for the Sunday flock, which we have undertaken to govern by the divine dispensation, and to supply the heavenly fodder with a healthy communication, especially to those who persist in the regions and villages under the prince of darkness's cunning persuasion, and are ignorant of the life of the way, and not of the things that are above, but what is below, they search with foolish instigation. But because certain nations exist in the parts of the North, who neither have the knowledge of God, nor have been reborn by the sacred wave of baptism, they exist under the shadow of death, and more creatures, which serve the Creator with an ignorant mind. Therefore, present most reverend brother and co-bishop Ebbo, necessary to the holy Church of Reims, with the consent of the faithful of God, we led them to address them in parts for the intimation of the truth. The confession of the Prince of the Apostles himself to evangelize by public authority, we handed over to everyone the ability to provide the word of life and the way of salvation everywhere, and to confirm the faith by heavenly education, and to corroborate the teaching of the Apostolic institution by repelling every diabolical error verbally. And if perhaps belonging to this divine his duty, some doubt has emerged, always resorting to God's holy Catholic and Apostolic Roman Church, and from its purest source he will draw, from which the divine grace intervening in the hearts of mortals can cleanse the harmful errors. Finally, having provided him with a colleague for the mission of this divine administration, we appointed the religious Halitgarius as a minister, as soon as he could reach the Apostolic see at the appropriate time to inform the Lord about the creditable business more easily performed, and never neglect himself in any part of the service committed to this authority of ours. There is no doubt that he will have to give an account before the district judge, and receive eternal punishments for his lost service. For which we remind all exhorters with one accord, for the love of Almighty God, and the veneration of our Lord Jesus Christ, and his Apostles. That in all the necessities of this legation you may be sure to comfort them with all your strength, and in the name of our Lord Jesus Christ, as it is written, "you should receive them; He who receives you", he says, receives me; and he who rejects you rejects me. And again: "What ye did unto one of the least of mine, ye did unto me." Whence we remind you more and more that, provided with devotion, and with a generous feeling of charity, with a pure mind, and with a sincere intention, and that you foresee all the necessities of this journey, you do not refrain from helping with pious kindness for your strength; that for a certain work of this piety you may receive from the Lord a merit worthy of retribution, or that you may be able to be numbered in the company of the saints as a compensatory function of this kind in the heavenly description. But if anyone, by the pious ecclesiastical counsel of the holy Catholic and Apostolic Church, has given consent or aid to this office of God for the intimidation of the nations, he shall, through the intervention of the blessed Apostles, also of the martyrs and all the saints, be credited with such merits in the heavenly joys. But if any one, contrary to what we wish, an adversary, insists on this divine worship, or has tried to hinder it in any way; To these, or to their co-operators, a reckless ministry should exist for this purpose, and by divine judgment and apostolic authority, he will be punished with the bond of anathema, and the guilty will be condemned to the devil's lot by perpetual condemnation.

Similarly, by the authority of this Apostolic privilege, Bishop Ansgar was attached to this legation with his associates, with the confirmation of Eugene, the next Pope; whom the succeeding Prince Gregory with the same encouragement ventured, and Simon the Archbishop with the priestly mantle of Ansgar alike decorated, in the Archbishop's dignity if not temporally wealthy, yet spiritually strengthened, extending the word of the Lord to the nations, the divine grace will prevail in them even the sublime would blush in all things.

Legatio Ebonis Archiepiscopi Remensis ad Gentes Septentrionales a Paschali Papa suscepta

Avtenticis per ordinem succedentium trium Apostolicorum roboratis privilegiis, Paschalis scilicet, Eugenii sive Gregorii sanctæ Romanæ sedis præsulum hoc legationis Christi exemplar editum cunctis Ecclesiæ catholicæ filiis porrectum atque præfixum, opem ferentibus, felicitatis negotium; impedientibus autem terribile damnationis judicium, si ligandi solvendique apostolicæ dignitatis verum Dei esse potest testimonium dicentis: Quodcunque ligaveris super terram, & reliqua. Insuper vero quod uni ex minimis meis fecistis, mihi fecistis; ut qui scandalizaverit unum de pusillis; vel cætera, mundo superbientibus divinitus vulgata tormenta. Piis tamen benignisque mentibus hæc ita conscripta, per ordinem firmaverunt inviolabilia jura apostolica.

Litera Pashcalis Papæ ad omnes Christianos Deo fideles

Paschalis Episcopus servus servorum Dei, universis sanctissimis fratribus, coëpiscopis, presbyteris, seu cæteris ecclesiasticis ordinibus gloriosissimisque Principibus, Ducibus, sive magnificis Comitibus, & cunctis Christianis Dei fidelibus. Cum religiosissimum constet curam ac sollicitudinem erga dominicum gregem gerere, quem divina dispensatione suscepimus gubernandum, atque coelestia pabula salubri communicatione subministrandum, maxime his, qui in competis & pagis sub principe tenebrarum callida suasione persistunt, & vitam viæ ignorantes devij, non quæ sursum sunt, sed quæ deorsum, stulta instigatione perquirunt. Sed quia in partibus Aquilonis quasdam gentes consistere, quæ nec dum agnitionem Dei habere, nec sacra unda baptismatis sunt renati, sub umbra mortis existere, & magis creaturæ quam creatori ignari mente servire cognovimus: Idcirco præsentem reverendissimum fratrem ac coëpiscopum nostrum Ebonem, sanctæ Remensis Ecclesiæ necessarium, cum consensu fidelium Dei, duximus illis in partibus pro intimatione veritatis dirigendum: quatinus auctoritate beatorum principum Apostolorum Petri ac Pauli nostra fraterna vice informatus, ante corpus & confessionem ipsius Apostolorum Principis evangelizandi publica auctoritate liberam tradidimus in omnibus facultatem, ut verbum vitæ viamque salutis ubique provideat, & fidei normam cœlesti educatione confirmet, atque Apo- stolicæ institutionis doctrinam omni diabolico errore depulso viva voce corroboret, & si fortasse ad hoc divinum pertinens officium aliquid dubium emerserit, ad sanctam Dei Catholicam atque Apostolicam Romanam Ecclesiam recurrendo semper, & ex ejus hauriet purissimo fonte latices, unde & a cordibus mortalium divina interveniente gratia noxis emundare possit errores. Collegam denique huic divinæ administrationis legationi ei providentes, Halitgarium religiosum adijcentes ministrum constituimus, quatinus ad sedem Apostolicam oportuno valeat tempore de credito negotio facilius præstante Domino intimare, & nunquam se in qualibet parte huic nostræ auctoritatis ministerio commisso negligere. Cui coram districto judice inde rationem reddere, & de destituto ministerio poenas recipere sempiternas, non dubium esse præfigimus. Pro quo omnes exhortantes unanimiter commonemus ob amorem omnipotentis Dei, & Domini nostri Iesu Christi, atque Apostolorum ejus venerationem; ut in omnibus necessitatibus legationis hujus totis viribus eis solatiari certetis, & in nomine Domini nostri Iesu Christi, sicut scriptum est, recipere debeatis; Qui vos, inquit, recipit, me recipit; & qui vos spernit, me spernit. Et iterum: Quod uni ex minimis meis fecistis, mihi fecistis. Vnde magis magisque commonemus, ut provida devotione, & largo caritatis affectu, puraque mente, ac sincera intentione, quæque itineri hujus necessaria prospicitis, pia benignitate pro viribus succurrere non renuatis; ut pro certo hujus pietatis opere participes apud Dominum dignæ retributionis meritum percipiatis, sive in cœlesti descriptione hujusmodi pro compensationis munere in consortio sanctorum connumerari valeatis. Si quis vero huic Dei officio ad intiminationem gentium a sancta catholica & Apostolica Ecclesia pio consultu ecclesiastico, destinato adsensum vel auxilium præbuerit, per interventionem beatorum Apostolorum, martyrum quoque atque sanctorum omnium in cœlestibus gaudiis talibus pro meritis mereatur adscribi. At vero si quis, quod non optamus, contrarius adversator, huic divino cultui institerit, vel in quoquam præpedire conatus fuerit; his, vel cooperatoribus eorum, ad hoc peragendum ministerium temerator extiterit, & divina jussione & Apostolica auctoritate, anathematis vinculo puniatur, & perpetua condemnatione reus, diabolica sorte damnetur.

In the name of our Lord God and Savior Jesus Christ. (834 AD)

Louis I the Pious, by the divine favor and propitiation of the clemency of the emperor Augustus. If the imperial authority shows that the special needs of each of our faithful must be looked into, how much more does this belong to the due and worthy providence of the generality. For the order of the Catholic and Apostolic Church, which Christ redeemed with his precious blood, and entrusted to us to govern and protect it, we must exercise a pious and solicitous care in all, and that in its advancement and exaltation we may show appropriate care to those who pertain to its need or utility and dignity things, let us provide new necessary and useful arrangements. Therefore, we want it to be certain to the children of the holy Church of God, present and future, how by divine ordaining grace, in our days, in the northern parts, in the nations of the Danes, that is to say, in the nations of the Danes, the great court of the heavenly grace of preaching and acquisition was revealed to Sueion, in such a way that the heavenly mysteries were converted from here and there to Christ, and ecclesiastical support would be desirable. Wherefore we praise our Lord our God, who, in our times and studies, has allowed the holy Church, namely his bride, to expand and advance in unknown places. Wherefore, together with the priests and the rest of the faithful of our Empire, seeing this cause worthy of God.

We thought it very necessary, and profitable to the dignity of the future Church, that we should choose a place more evidently suited to our borders, where we would establish the archbishop's seat, as ordered by our authority. Wherefore all those barbarous nations were able to take the fodder and abundance of eternal life, and being thirsty, they had before their hands and eyes the grace of salvation. Moreover, even the ceremonies of our great ancestors would never fail in our efforts to gain in our days. Indeed, our father, Charles of glorious memory, subjected all Saxony to the ecclesiastical religion, and taught the yoke of Christ to the borders of the Danes and the Slavs, forbidding the ferocious hearts of the Danes and Slavs with iron, where between these two nations of the Danes, or the Vandals, the last part of Saxony was situated, and perceiving that various dangers, namely temporal and spiritual, lay between them. He decided to make en episcopal seat there across Albia. Hence, after the land of the Nordalbings had been loosened by captivity, which they had suffered for seven years because of much perfidy committed in the very beginnings of Christianity, so that that place might not be invaded by the barbarians. Count Ecbert had ordered it, as he no longer wished to entrust that place to the neighboring bishops. But lest any of them should afterwards claim this parish for himself, he sent a certain bishop, named Amalarius, from remote parts of Gaul, to consecrate the first church there. But with his pious generosity he specially took care to assign to him the sacred relics of the same Church, and several ecclesiastical gifts. Afterward, however, the captives converging from all sides to the desired country, he specially commended the same parish to a certain priest named Heridac, whom the whole Church of Nordalbing, lest it should be drawn back to the rites of the gentiles, or because that place seemed most suitable for gaining these nations, had arranged to be consecrated an Archbishop, so that he himself, on the occasion or with the highest authority, in the very borders of the Gentiles diligently preaching, the holy Church would be multiplied, while the care of the neighbors of the very new bishops was not sufficient to run through everything. He also delegated to the same presbyter a certain cell called Hrodnace, inasmuch as the same place would be filled with dangers on all sides. But since the consecration of the man I have already mentioned, the speedy passage from this light of the pious parent took place in his days, but I, whom divine clemency had brought to the seat of his kingdom, when I insisted on the various affairs of the kingdom, this also the aforesaid study of my father, as in the kingdom. I had paid less careful attention to the completion of the ends, and at the persuasion of some I transferred the aforesaid cell to the same monastery, while in the meantime I commended the neighboring parish to the neighboring bishops. And now, both because of the above-mentioned ecclesiastical gains demonstrated among the nations, and because of the vow of our pious Father, that nothing of his study should remain incomplete, we establish, together with the ecclesiastical consent, the aforesaid last in the region of Saxony beyond Albia in a place called Hamburg with the whole province of the Nordalbings of the proper Church to set up an archiepiscopal seat with vigor, to preside over it for the first time and to be solemnly consecrated by the hands of Drogo of Metz, and we made Ansgar the most holy and palatial dignitary of Ansgar, in the presence of the archbishops of Ebbo of Reims, Hetti of Treviri, and Ottgar of Mainz, together with many other generals assembled in the assembly of the princes of our whole empire; and with the consent and consecration of the Bishops of Helingandus and Willericus, from whom we have received the parts already mentioned, which we once communicated to them. By the summoning of the Gentiles, or by the redemption of the captives, or by the filling of the same See surrounded by many dangers, or by the Consolation of those who were fighting for God there, for the love of God, we entrust him to Sixtus the Confessor in perpetuity. We also desire that the property of the aforesaid See, and of the aforesaid monastery, under the most complete defense and protection of immunity, may be established and protected: so that no public judge, or any other person endowed with public power, may, from their possessions, impose taxes, tributes, mansions, or preparations, or tolls, or trusts. to remove their officers, or to tear off their men, such as the coasts and natives, remaining on their land, nor presume to demand or demand any public functions, or bribes, or illicit opportunities. But that it may be permitted to the aforesaid archbishop and his successors, and to all the clergy appointed under his rule, to dwell quietly in the service of God, and to invoke divine mercy for us, our law, and the state of our entire empire. And in order that this authority might obtain a perpetual firmness by its own strength, we confirmed it with our own hand, and ordered it to be sealed with the impression of our ring.

The sign of the most pious Emperor Louis I.

I recognized Hirminmarus the Notary at the turn of Theodon. Given on the 1st of May, in the year of Christ, the propitiation of the 21st reign of the Lord Louis, by the indictment of the pious Augustus the 12th year, this act given at Aachen in the royal palace in the name of God was successful. Amen.

In nomine Domini Dei & Salvatoris nostri Jesu Christi.

Ludovicus divina favente & propitiante Clementia Imperator Augustus. Si specialibus cujusque fidelium nostrorum necessitatibus perspectis subveniendum esse Imperialis auctoritas monstrat, quantum magis ad debitam generalitatis providentiam xquum dignumque pertinet. Ut & Ecclesiæ Catholicæ atque Apostolicæ, quam Christus suo pretioso sanguine redimit, eamque nobis regendam tuen- damque commisit, piam ac sollicitam in cunctis oportet gerere curam, & ut in ejus provectu & exaltatione congruam exhibeamus diligentiam novis ad ejus necessitatem vel utilitatem atque dignitatem pertinentibus rebus, nova imo necessaria & utilia provideamus constituta. Idcirco sanctæ Dei Ecclesiæ filiis præsentibus & futuris certum esse volumus qualiter divina ordinante gratia, nostris in diebus, Aquilonaribus in partibus, in gentibus videlicet Danorum, Sueonum magnum coelestis gratiæ prædicationis sive acquisitionis patefecit atrium, ita ut mustitudo hinc inde ad Christum conversa, mysteria coelestia, Ecclesiasticaque subsidia desiderabiliter expeteret. Unde Domino Deo nostro laudes immensas persolventes extollimus, qui nostris temporibus ac studiis, sanctam Ecclesiam, sponsam videlicet suam, in locis ignotis siuit dilatari atque proficere. Quamobrem una cum Sacerdotibus cæterisque Imperii nostri fidelibus hanc Deo dignam cernentes causam valde necessariam, atque futuræ Ecclesiæ dignitati proficuam dignum esse duximus, ut locum aptum nostris in finibus evidentius eligeremus, ubi sedem Archiepiscopalem per hoc nostræ auctoritatis præceptum statueremus. Unde omnes illæ barbara nationes æternæ vitæ pabulum uberiusque capere valerent, & sitientes salutis gratia præ manibus oculisque haberent. Insuper etiam & magnorum Progenitorum nostrorum sacra lucrandi studio nostris in diebus nunquam deficerent. Genitor etenim noster gloriosa memoriæ Karulus omnem Saxoniam Ecclesiasticæ religioni subdidit, jugumque Christi ad usque terminos Danorum atque Slavorum corda ferocia ferro perdomans docuit, ubi inter has utrasque gentes Danorum videlicet sive Wandalorum ultimam Saxoniæ partem sitam, & diversis periculis, temporalibus videlicet ac spiritualibus interjacentem perspiciens, pontificalem ibidem sedem fieri decrevit trans Albiam. Unde postquam terram Nordalbingorum laxata captivitate, quam ob multam perfidiam in ipsis Christianitatis initiis patratam per septennium passi sunt, ne locus ille a barbaris invaderetur Ecberto Comiti restituere præceperat, non jam vicinis Episcopis locum illum committere voluit . Sed ne quisquam eorum hanc sibi deinceps Parochiam vindicaret, ex remotis

Galliæ partibus, quendam Episcopum, Amalarium nomine, direxit, qui primitivam ibidem Ecclesiam consecraret. Sed ei eidem Ecclesiæ sacras reliquias, ac plura Ecclesiastica munera pia largitate specialiter destinare curavit. Postmodum vero captivis ad optatam patriam undique confluentibus, eandem parochiam cuidam presbytero Heridac nomine specialiter commendavit, quem universæ Nordalbingorum Ecclesiæ, ne ad ritum relaberetur gentilium, vel quia locus ille lucrandis ad- huc gentibusvidebatur aptissimus disposuerat consecrari Archiepiscopum, ut ipsi occasione vel autoritate summa, in ipsis terminis gentium sedulitate prædicandi, sancta multiplicaretur Ecclesia dum vicinorum ipsius novitatis Episcoporum multa latitudinis cura non sufficiebat discurrere per omnia. Delegavit etiam eidem presbytero quandam cellam Hrodnace vocatam, quatenus eidem loco periculis undique circumdatodnace fieret plementum. Sed quia consecrationem jam dicti viri, velox ex hac luce transitus pii genitoris in diebus ejus fieri perhibuit, ego autem quem divina clementia in sedem regni ejus asciverat, cum in diversis regni negotiis insisterem hoc quoque prædictum patris mei studium, velut regniin finibus peractum minus caute attenderem, suadentibus quibusdam jam dictam cellam ad idem monasterium contuli , vicinam vero parochiam vicinis Episcopis interim commendavi. Nunc autem, tam propter suprascripta Ecclesiastica lucra in gentibus demonstrata , quam & propter votum pii Genitoris nostri, ne quid ejus studii imperfectum remaneat, statuimus una cum consensu Ecclesiastico, præfata ultima in regione Saxonia trans Albiam in loco nuncupato Hammaburg cum universa Nordalbingorum provincia Ecclesiæ proprii vigoris constituere sedem Archiepiscopalem, cui ad primum præesse atque solenniter consecrari per manus Drogonis Metensis, & summæ sanctæque palatinæ dignitatis Angsgar fecimus Archiepiscopum astantibus Archiepiscopis Ebone Remensi, Hetti Trevirensi & Ottgare Moguntiensi cum plurimis aliis generali in conventu totius Imperii nostri Præsulibus congregatis: assistentibus quoque specialiter & consentientibus atque consecrantibus Helingando & Willcrico Episcopis, a quibus jam dictæ partes a nobis sibi olim communicatas recepimus. Cui videlicet Ansgario, quia præfatis in Gentibus, hæc nostris in diebus dignissima in vocatione Gentilium vel redemtione captivorum monstrata sunt lucra, tam nostra, quam sanctæ Romanæ Ecclesiæ auctoritate, hanc Deo dignam in gentibus commisimus legationem ac proprii vigoris adscribere decrevimus dignitatem. Et ut hæc nova constructio periculosis in his locis cœpta subsistere valeat, (ne prævalente Barbarorum sævitia deperiret) quandam cellam Turholt vocatam huic novæ constructioni, quam suæ Archiepiscopi successorumque suorum in gentibus Legationi perenniter servituram, ad nostram nostræque sobolis perpetuam mercedem, divinæ obtulimus Majestati. Homines quoque, qui ejusdem cellæ beneficia habere videntur, ab omni expeditione, vel militia, sive qualibet occupatione liberamus, ut idem Venerabilis Episcopus ad hanc Deo dignam in provisis temporibus Legationem nullum in hoc patiatur impedimentum. Dona vero , quæ ex eadem cella nostris partibus dare solebant, & nobis quoque succes- soribusque nostris similiter dari volumus. His exceptis, majus minusque in convocatione Paganorum, vel redemtione, captivorum sive ejusdem Sedis plemento multimodis periculis circumdato vel ibidem Deo militantium Solatio, ob amorem Dei ac b. Sixti Confessoris ejus perpetuo delegamus. Res quoque præfatæ Sedis, & jam dicti monasterii sub plenissima defensione & immunitatis tuitione volumus, ut consistant ac tueantur: ita , ut nullus judex publicus aut alia quælibet potestate publica prædita persona, de eorum rebus fredum, tributa, mansionaticos vel paratas aut teloneum vel fidei jussores tollere aut homines ipsorum tam litos qvam & ingenuos, super terram eorum manentes distringere, nec ullas publicas functiones, aut redibitiones, vel illicitas occasiones requirere vel exigere præsumat. Sed, ut liceat venerabili Archiepiscopo prædicto suisque successoribus, ac omni Clero sub eorundem regimine constituto, quiete in Dei servitio degere & pro nobis leque nostra atque statu totius imperii nostri divinam misericordiam exorare. Et ut hæc auctoritas sui vigoris perpetuam obtineat firmitatem, manu propria subter eam firmavimus, & annuli nostri impressione signare jussimus .

Signum Hlodewici piissimi Imperatoris.

Hirminmarus Notarius ad vicem Theodonis recognovi. Data Idus Mai, Anno Christo propitio XXI imperii Domini Hlodiwici piissimi Augusti Indictione XII , Actum Aquisgrani in palatio Regio in Dei nomine feliciter. Amen.

For the recognition of all the faithful (835 AD)

Bishop Gregory, the servant of the servants of God, we want to be certain of the recognition of all the faithful, how the most excellent king Charles of blessed memory, inspired by the divine spirit in the time of our predecessors, subjected the Saxon nation to the sacred worship, and the yoke of Christ, which is sweet and light, even to the borders of the Danes and the Slavs fierce hearts he taught to pardon the sword, and the last part of his kingdom was established across Albia amid the deadly dangers of the pagans. That is to say that he should not revert to the rites of the gentiles, or else, because he seemed to be most apt to gain the nations, he had decided to found a cathedral with his own vigor. But because death had prevented the effect on the succession of his most excellent son, Louis, the emperor Augustus. He effectively fulfilled the pious devotion of his holy parent. What account has been reported to us by the venerable Bishops Ratolph and Arnold, as well as Count Geroldus and the venerable messenger, to be confirmed. We, therefore, knowing all the providence established there worthy of God, and having also the presence of our brother and son Ansgar, the first Archbishop of Nordalbing consecrated by the hands of Drogo, Bishop of Metz, have resolved to strengthen the holy study of the great emperors. Both by the present authority and also by the giving of the mantle, in the manner of our predecessors, inasmuch as so much established by authority, our aforesaid son, and his successors, who persist in winning over the people against the temptations of the devil, are stronger, and our son himself, who has already been mentioned, Ansgar, and his successors, ambassadors in all the surrounding nations of the Danes, the Sveoni, (Norwegians, Farrix, Grønlandan, Halsingolandan, Icelanders, Scridevindu, Slavorum, nay, nor all the Northern and Eastern nations in any way named). And placing the head and breast upon the body and confession of St. Peter the Apostle, we grant to him and his successors the authority to keep our turn forever, and to evangelize the public, and we decree that the very seat of the Nordalbings, called Hamburg, be consecrated in honor of the Holy Savior and his immaculate mother Mary, be Archbishop. As for the consecration of succeeding priests, until the number of consecrators from the gentiles increases, we entrust the sacred palace of providence in the meantime. Indeed, the person of a vigorous preacher, and suitable for such an office, is always chosen in succession, but all those assigned by the venerable prince to this office worthy of God, we also confirm his pious wishes by our pious authority; and with perpetual revenge we condemn the guilty to the diabolical lot, so that we may defend the Apostolic summit more securely from adverse parties on either side, zealously zealous for the cause of God with pious affection, after the manner of our predecessors. And because the divine clemency has arranged for you, dearest son of Ansgar, to be the first archbishop in the new seat, and we give the mantle to celebrate the solemnities of the masses, which we bestow on you in your days, to use and to use the privileges that remain in your Church's perpetual state. May the Holy Trinity deign to preserve your life unscathed, and after the bitterness of the age lead you to everlasting happiness. Amen.

LETTERS FROM THE NORTH

Omnium fidelium dignoscentiae

Gregorius Episcopus, servus servorum Dei, omnium fidelium dignoscentiæ certum esse volumus, qualiter beatæ memoriæ præcellentissimus Rex Karolus tempore prædecessorum nostrorum divino afflatus spiritu, gentem Saxonum sacro cultui subdidit, jugumque Christi, qvod suave ac leve est, ad usque terminos Danorum sive Slavorum corda ferocia ferro perdomans docuit, ultimamque regni ipsius partem trans Albiam inter mortifera paganorum pericula constitutam, videlicet ne ad ritum relaberetur gentilium, vel etiam, quia lucrandis adhuc gentibus aptissima videbatur, proprio Episcopali vigore fundare decreverat. Sed quia mors effectum prohibuerat, succedente ejus præcellentissimo filio Hludewico Imperatore Aug. pium studium sacri genitoris sui efficaciter implevit. Qvæ ratio nobis per venerabiles Ratolfum sive Vernoldum Episcopos, nec non Geroldum comitem vel missum venerabilem relata est confirmanda. Nos igitur omnem ibi Deo dignam statutam providentiam cognoscentes, instructi etiam præsentia fratris filiique nostri Ansgar, primi Nordalbingorum Archiepiscopi per manus Drogonis Metensis Episcopi consecrati, sanctum studium magnorum Imperatorum, tam præsenti auctoritate, quam etiam pallii datione, more prædecessorum nostrorum roborare decrevimus, quatenus tanta auctoritate fundatus prædictus filius noster, ejusque successores lucrandis plebibus insistentes adversus tentamenta Diaholi, validiores existant, ipsumque filium nostrum jam dictum Ansgar & successores ejus legatos in omnibus circumquaque gentibus Danorum, Sveonum, (Nortwehorum, Farrix, Gronlandan, Halsingolandan, Islandan, Scridevindum, Slavorum, nec nec non omnium Septentrionalium & Orientalium nationum quocunque modo nominatarum) delegamus. Et posito capite & pectore super corpus & confessionem sancti Petri Apostoli, sibi suisque successoribus vicem nostram perpetuo retinendam, publicamque evangelizandi tribuimus auctoritatem, ipsamque sedem Nordalbingorum, Hammaborch dictam, in honore sancti Salvatoris, ejusque intemeratæ genitricis Mariæ consecratam, Archiepiscopalem esse decernimus. Consecrationem vero succedentium sacerdotum donec consecrantium numerus ex gentibus augeatur, sacræ palatine pro- videntiæ interim committimus. Strenui vero prædicatoris persona, tantoque officio apta in successione semper eligatur, omnia vero a venerabili Principe ad hoc Deo dignum officium deputata nostra etiam auctoritate pia ejus vota firmamus, omnemque resistentem vel contradicentem, atque piis nostris his studiis quolibet modo insidiantem, anathematis muerone percutimus, atque perpetua ultione reum diabolica sorte damnamus, ut culmen Apostolicum more prædecessorum nostrorum causam Dei pio affectu zelantes ab adversis hinc inde partibus tutius muniamus. Et quia te, charissime fili Ansgar, Divina clementia nova in sede primum disposuit esse Archiepiscopum, nosque pallium ad missarum solemnia celebranda tribuimus, quod tibi in diebus tuis, uti & Ecclesiæ tuæ perpetuo statu manentibus privilegiis uti largimur. Sancta Trinitas vitam tuam conservare dignetur incolumen, atque post seculi amaritudinem ad perpetuam perducat beatitudinem; Amen.

Since Apostolic dignity
(846 AD)

Bishop Sergius, servant of the servants of God, to the most blessed Ansgar, Archbishop of the Church of Hamburg, God's grace forever.

Since it is the Apostolic dignity not only to found Churches, but also to sublimate those founded by other spiritual architects of Churches, we thought it worthy, dearest brother, to incline the ears due to your dignity to your request. We grant you, therefore, as was granted by our predecessor, the blessed Gregory, namely, that the nations of the Vimodians, Norblings, Danes, Norwegians, Swedes, or any of the northern nations should be submitted to the yoke of faith by your preaching, to possess the see of Hamburg under spiritual dominion, and to all your successors, to leave the same seat to possess forever. We also decree for you and all your successors at the seat of Hamburg to have the use of the mantle on the feasts and times named for you by our predecessor, namely on Easter, on Pentecost, on the Nativity of the Lord, on the Assumption, on the Nativity, on the purification of Saint Mary, on the birthdays of the Apostles and on Sundays on the days and all the festivals celebrated in your diocese, your head should also be adorned with a mitre, and a cross should be carried before you. Come, then, most blessed brother, the good work which you have begun, and do not stop until you are successful, found churches in suitable places, consecrate priests, and according to determined terms ordain bishops, of all of whom you are the archbishop, and all the aforesaid nations will further benefit the bishops with the people who are subject to you and to all your successors at the seat of Hamburg, may they continue in perpetual subjection and obedience to the subject. Moreover, we confirm to you and to the holy Church of Hamburg and to all your successors by Apostolic authority, whatever your Churches have already been handed over by Christians, or have been further delegated in parishes, in estates, in all things, movable or immovable, in the possessions of both sexes, as the said church to possess inviolable power forever. But if anyone tries to go against the privilege of our authority, and in any way attempts to break it in part or in whole, even if he is a person of Apostolic dignity, let him perish by eternal excommunication with Judas, the betrayer of the Lord, unless he repents and satisfies the Church of Hamburg. And the observer of this admonition and judgment may have the blessing of Almighty God, the blessed Apostles, and ours, who act as their Vicar. May the Holy Trinity deign to keep your fraternity safe at all times, and after the bitterness of this age lead to eternal happiness. Given by the hand of Leo the Chancellor of the Holy Roman Church in the month of April, the ninth indictment.

Quum Apostolicæ dignitatis

Sergius Episcopus, servus servorum Dei, beatissimo Anschario sanctæ Hammaburgensis Ecclesiæ Archiepiscopo gratiam Dei in perpetuum.

Quum Apostolicæ dignitatis est non solum Ecclesias fundare, sed & ab aliis Ecclesiarum spiritualibus architectis fundatas sublimare, dignum duximus, frater charissime, pro petitionis tuæ voto aures debitas dignitatis tuæ inclinare. Concedimus igitur tibi, sicut a prædecessore nostro beato Gregorio Concessum est, scilicet, ut gentes Vimodiorum, Norblingorum, Danorum, Noruenorum, Suenorum, vel quascunque septentrionalium nationum jugo fidei prædicatione tua subdideris, ad sedem Hammaburgensem spirituali dominatione possideas, & omnibus successoribus tuis, ad eandem sedem perpetuo possidendas relinquas. Decernimus quoque tibi & omnibus successoribus tuis ad sedem Hammaburgensem usum pallii habendum in festis & temporibus a prædecessore nostro tibi denominatis, scilicet in Pascha, in Pentecosten, in natali Domini, in assumtione, in nativitate, in purificatione sanctæ Mariæ, in nataliciis Apostolorum & dominicis diebus & omnibus festis in diœcesi tua celebribus, ornari quoque caput tuum mitra, portare ante te crucem. Age ergo, frater beatissime, opus bonum, quod incoepisti, nec desistas donec proficias, funda in locis oportunis Ecclesias, consecra presbyteros, & per disterminatos terminos ordina Episcopos, quorum omnium tu Archiepiscopus existas, omnesque supradictarum nationum amplius profuturi Episcopi cum subjectis sibi plebibus tibi & omnibus successoribus tuis ad sedem Hammaburgensem perpetua subjectione & obedientia subjecti permaneant. Præterea tibi & sanctæ Hammaburgensi Ecclesiæ & omnibus successoribus tuis auctoritate Apostolica firmamus, quæcunque Ecclesiæ tuæ jam a Christicolis tradita sunt, vel amplius delegata fuerint in parochiis, in prædiis, in omnibus rebus, mobilibus vel immobilibus, in mancipiis utriusque sexus, ut ea Ecclesia prædicta inviolabili potestate perpetuo possideat. Si quis autem contra hujus nostræ auctoritatis privilegium ire temptaverit, & quoquo modo in parte vel in toto frangere nisus fuerit, etiam si sit Apostolicæ dignitatis persona, æterna excommunicatione cum Juda traditore Domini pereat, nisi resipiscat, & Ecclesiæ Hammaburgensi satisfaciat. Observator autem hujus amonicionis & jussionis habeat benedictionem omnipotentis Dei, beatorum Apostolorum & nostram, qui eorum fungimur Vicariatione. Sancta Trinitas fraternitatem tuam omni tempore conservare dignetur incolumen, atque post hujus seculi amaritudinem ad perpetuam perducat beatitudinem. Data per manum Leonis Cancellarii sanctæ Romanæ Ecclesiæ in mense Aprili, indictione nona.

Worthy of Exaltation
(March 12, 849 AD)

Leo the Bishop, the servant of the servants of God, to the Archbishop Ansgar of the Holy Church of Hamburg, the eternal bliss of life.

We thought it worthy of exaltation, dearest brother, to incline the ears of your due kindness to your pious request. We grant you, therefore, as was granted by our predecessor, the blessed Gregory, namely, that the nations of the Wimodians, Norblings, Danes, Norwegians, Swedes, or any of the northern nations, may be submitted to the yoke of faith by your preaching. What follows corresponds verbatim to Sergius the Bull, down to the words: 'Let the Church of Hammaburg be satisfied'. Given by the hand of Stephen the Chancellor of the Holy Roman Church in the month of March the 12th Indictment.

Sublimare dignum

Leo Episcopus, servus servorum Dei, Anschario sanctæ Hammaburgensis Ecclesia Archiepiscopo, æternæ vitae beatitudinem Quoniam Apostolicæ dignitatis est, non solum Ecclesias fundare, sed & ab aliis Ecclesiarum spiritualibus architectis fundatas. Sublimare, dignum duximus, frater charissime, pio petitionis tuæ voto aures debitæ benignitatis tuæ inclinare. Concedimus igitur tibi , sicut a prædecessore nostro beato Gregorio concessum est, scilicet ut gentes Wimodiorum, Norblingorum, Danorum, Norvenorum, Svenorum vel qvascunqve septentrionalium nationum jugo fidei prædicatione tua subdideris. Quæ sequuntur verbotenus correspondent Bullæ Sergi usque ad verba : Ecclesiæ Hammaburgensi satisfaciat. Data per manum Stephani Cancellarii sanctæ Romanæ Ecclesiæ mense Martio Indictione XII.

Anyone who knows the Lord
(May 31, 858 AD)

Nicholas the bishop, servant of the servants of God, to all the faithful of the holy Church of God present, that is to say, the salvation of the time and the future and the Apostolic blessing.

Whoever does not doubt that our Lord and Redeemer, Jesus Christ, came down from the bosom of the Father to the earth in order to demonstrate to the hearts of men the truth and certain faith, certainly does not ignore all who have become partakers of the same faith through his grace, and especially us, who from the first have so much power, that We hold that the minister has the most important place, that he should insist on winning for men, and that he should sow the seeds of the word throughout all nations, and minister to those who sow comfort. And now, because Louis the Most High King, through Salomon, the venerable Bishop of the City of Constantia, endeavored to inform the Apostolate, that in pious memory Louis the Emperor, his father, had taken a certain monk, named Anscharius, from the monastery of Corbeja, and placed him near the river Albia, on the borders of the Danes and Slavs, and in the castle of the Saxons. Hammaburg between the two Episcopates of Breman and Verden, of which by taking away the Churches and tithes for the support of the cause of the aforesaid bishop and his Clerics he condoned in the aforesaid place nodding, and granting the solemnity of the Apostolic See privileges to our predecessor in blessed memory Pope Gregory, by whose authority also the see was established in the aforesaid people of Nordalbing he is the archbishopric in the above-mentioned castle of Hamburg. And in the same seat the Archbishop, having received the mantle from the Apostolic See, was the first to be ordained Ansgar, to whom the aforesaid priest delegated the care of sowing the word of God and winning souls to God, whose delegation and authority and acceptance of the mantle we have a page from our aforesaid son Louis, by the king, by the aforesaid Solomon, the most holy bishop was destined, according to the custom of the holy Roman Church. By the tenor of which in the pages we find that this was so, as the mercy of the aforesaid king intimated to us through the faithful man Salomon, that is, the bishop. Wherefore we, following in the footsteps of the great Pope, and our Predecessor, Gregory, and recognizing all the providence established there worthy of God, the wish of the great princes, that is to say, of Louis the rich memory of Augustus, and his equivocal son the most excellent King. Both by the precept of this Apostolic authority, and also by the giving of the Pallium, according to the manner of our predecessors we decided to strengthen, inasmuch as the pre-named Ansgar, the first bishop of the Nordalbings, and after him his successors, who were founded on such authority, persisted in gaining the people, were stronger against the temptations of the devil. Our own son Ansgar, as I have already said, in all the surrounding nations of the Swedes or Danes, nor even of the Slavs or in the rest, wherever divine piety has opened the door to them in the established parts, we grant the public power and authority to evangelize, and the very seat of the Nordalbings called Hamburg, in honor of the holy savior and his We decree that Mary, consecrated to the ever-virgin, unblemished mother, will henceforth be Archbishop. And that, after the death of the energetic preacher bishop, oft-mentioned Archbishop Ansgar, a person and a successor fit for such a duty should always be chosen, under the testimony of divine judgment. True, because Charles the king, the brother of the often-mentioned king, after the death of the emperor, his father, in pious memory of Louis I, removed from the above-named place, which is called the Monastery of Hamburg, which is called Turholt, as it seemed that after the partition between his brothers, he should lie in his kingdom, situated in Western France, which his father had given there for the supply and sustenance of the bishop and his clergy. To begin, as it is reported, all the Ministers of the altar withdrew, since they failed to take the necessary things, they withdrew from them to the gentiles, and the same Legation to the gentiles failed by this act, and the city of Hamburg itself became deserted. Therefore, while these things were being done, the bishop of the diocese, which is said to be contiguous to this one, died. When the said king saw the said diocese vacant and that new constitution failing, and moreover both of these churches, God permitting the secret judgment, greatly weakened by the savagery of the barbarians, he began to complain, how the aforesaid church of Bremen, in the novel said, should be united to the archbishopric, and submitted to the see, by a decree confirming this wish of ours: whence by the fence named the venerable Missus, namely Salomon, bishop of the city of Constantia. This was reported to us to be confirmed and requested to be confirmed by our authority. We, therefore, having carefully weighed the examination, observed that, because of the urgent need, and the gains of souls shown among the nations, it would be useful. We have not doubted that everything which is proved profitable to the Church exists, and does not result from divine precepts, that it is permissible and should be done, especially in such a new planting of Christianity, in which various events usually happen. Wherefore, by the authority of Almighty God, and of the blessed Apostles Peter and Paul, and by this decree of ours, we have decreed, according to the wish of the Most Reverend king Louis, that the aforesaid dioceses of Hamburg, namely Bremen, and henceforth not to be two but one, and to be called, and to sit under the decree of our predecessor, the Archbishop it is functionally sublimated, having been restored only from the affairs of the Church of Bremen to the Bishopric of Werden, having been removed from it. But no Archbishop of Cologne will claim for himself any power in the same diocese. Therefore, let us and all the true worshipers of religion be exhorted, that the sacraments may be a helper and comfort to those who serve in this mission, inasmuch as they deserve to receive the full reward of this favor from him who said: "Go, teach all nations, and whoever receives you receives me too". Therefore, all things assigned by our beloved son king Louis to this service worthy of God, we also confirm his pious wishes by authority. And because the accidents of the past make us cautious for the future, we strike with the beak of anathema anyone who opposes or contradicts and in any way insinuates our studies, and condemns to the devil's lot the guilty of perpetual revenge: as the Apostolic summit in the manner of our predecessors, and the cause of God, zealous with affection, let us defend ourselves more securely from the adverse parties on either side. And since the divine clemency, dearest son of Ansgar, has arranged for you to be the archbishop for the first time in the new seat, and we give you the mantle to celebrate the solemnities of the masses, which we bestow on you in your days, and the privileges that remain in your Church's perpetual state, as we bestow upon you, the honor of this dress must be preserved by the vivacity of manners. If, therefore, the shepherds of the sheep guard their flocks in the sun and frost, lest any of them should perish either by wandering, or by the woolly bites of wild beasts, looking round with ever-watchful eyes, how much sweat and how much care ought we, who are called shepherds of souls, to be vigilant, and to attend to the duty undertaken we advise you to be somewhat involved in earthly affairs. Let your life therefore be a way for your children, in it, if there is any crookedness in them, let them direct it: in it, what they imitate, look, in it always considering, let them make progress, so that your life after God may be seen as good. Let not thy heart, therefore, be lifted up by good things which are temporarily flattered, nor cast down by adversity: let them know the district of evil, let the pious and benevolent abound, let not another's malice make the innocent blameless before thee, let grace not excuse the guilty, let thy defense come to the aid of widows and orphans unjustly oppressed. Behold, dearest brother, among many other things these are the priesthood, these are the mantles, which if you diligently keep, what you show that you have received outside, you will have inside. In truth, know that all these things annexed above have been canceled by the Apostolic See of Your Beatitude, if you have in any way deviated at all from the faith and decrees of the holy Catholic and Apostolic Roman Church. But if you presume willingly to deviate from the faith and institutions or sanctions of the Apostolic See with such exalted honor, you will be deprived of these benefits which we have bestowed upon you. Moreover, we allow you to wear the mantle, not except according to the manner of your Apostolic See, namely, that your successors, by themselves or by their Ambassadors and the writings, keep the faith with us, and receive the six holy Synods, and the decrees of all the Roman See Presulum, and the letters that were brought to him have been, he must reverently observe and perform all his days in writing and by oath.

Written by the hand of Zachariah the Notary in the Holy Roman Church, in the month of May, indictment 6. Good health. Given the day before the month of June, by the hand of Tiberius Primicerius of the holy Apostolic See.

Quisquis Dominum

Nicolaus episcopus, servus servorum Dei, omnibus fidelibus sancte Dei Ecclesiæ præsentis scilicet temporis et futuri salutem et Apostolicam benedictionem.

Quisquis Dominum et Redemtorem nostrum Jesum Christum de sinu Patris, ad terram, pro demonstranda cordibus hominum vera & certa fide descendisse non dubitat, profecto non ignorat, omnes, qui ejusdem fidei per gratiam ipsius participes facti sunt & precipue Nos, qui per primum tante virtutis Ministrum locum precipuum tenemus hominibus debere lucrandis insistere & per universas gentes verbi semina serere & solatio serentibus ministrare . Nunc autem, quia Ludovicus sublimissimus Rex per Salomonem venerabilem Episcopum Civitatis Constantie nostro studuit Apostolatui intimare, quod pie memorie Ludowicus Imperator genitor suus, quendam Monachum, nomine Anscharium de monasterio Corbeja tulisset & collocasset eum juxta Albiam fluvium in confinibus Danorum & Slavorum, Saxonumque in castello Hammaburg inter duos Episcopatus Bremon & Verden, de quibus tollens Ecclesias & decimas ad sustentationem provehendi caussa præfati Episcopi Clericorumque ejus condonasset in predicto loco annuente, ac solemnia sedis Apostolica privilegia prebente predecessore nostro beate memorie Papa Gregorio, cujus etiam auctoritate in supradicto Nordalbingorum populo sedes constituta est Archiepiscopalis in castello superius memorato Hammaburg; & in eadem quoque sede Archiepiscopus, accepto a sede Apostolica pallio, primus est ordinatus Ansgarius, cui a prefato Pontifice delegata est cura seminandi verbum Dei & animas lucrandi Deo, cujus de- legationis & auctoritatis & Pallii acceptionis pagina nobis est a præfato filio nostro Ludovico Rege per jam dictum Salomonem sanctissimum Episcopum destinata, juxta morem sancte Romane Ecclesie ebullata; per cujus tenorem pagine hec ita fuisse comperimus, sicut pietas nobis jam prefati Regis per fidelem virum Salomonem scilicet Episcopum intimavit. Unde nos vestigia tanti Pontificis & Prædecessoris nostri sequentes Gregorii, omnemque ibi Deo dignam statutam providentiam agnoscentes, magnorum Principum votum, Ludovici videlicet dive recordationis Augusti, & equivoci ejus filii excellentissimi Regis, tam hujus Apostolice auctoritatis precepto, quam etiam Pallii datione, more Predecessorum nostrorum roborare decrevimus. Quatenus tanta fundatus auctoritate prenominatus Ansgarius, primus Nordalbingorum Episcopus, &

post ipsum successores ejus lucrandis plebibus insistentes, adversus tentamenta diaboli validiores existant; ipsumque filium nostrum jam dictum Ansgarium in omnibus circumquaque Gentibus Sueorum sive Danorum, nec non etiam Slavorum vel in ceteris, ubicunque illis in partibus constitutis divina pietas ostium aperuerit, publicam Evangelizandi tribuimus pótestatem & auctoritatem, ipsamque sedem Nordalbingorum Hammaburg dictam, in honorem sancti salvatoris ejusque intemerate genetricis, semper virginis, Marie consecratam, Archiepiscopalem decernimus deinceps esse. Atque, ut strenui prædicatoris Episcopi post decessum crebro dicti Ansgarii Archiepiscopi, persona, tantoque officio apta eligatur semper successio , sub divini judicii obtestatione statuimus. Verum, quia Karolus Rex, sæpe dicti Regis frater post decessum Imperatoris, patris sui , pie memorie Ludovici I. abstulit a prenominato loco , qui dicitur Hammaburg Monasterium, quod appcllatur Turholt, utpote quod post partitionem inter fratres suos, in Regno suo conjacere videbatur, situm in Occidentali Francia, quod illic genitor suus ad supplementum & victum Episcopo & Clerisis ejus dederat; cœpere, sicut fertur, omnes Ministri altaris recedere, deficientibus quippe necessariis sumtibus, ab ipsis recesserunt gentibus, & eadem ad Gentes Legatio, per hujusmodi factum defecit, ipsaque Metropolis Hammaburg deserta facta est. Igitur dum hæc agerentur mortuus est Dioeceseos Episcopus, quæ huic contigua esse dicitur: cumque sepe dictus Rex & hanc Diocesin vacantem & illam novellam constitutionem cerneret deficientem, insuper utramque hanc Ecclesiam, Dei permitente occulto judicio, per barbarorum sevitiam admodum attenuatam, querere cepit, qualiter predicta Bremensis Ecclesia, novelle dicte Archiepiscopali uniretur, ac subderetur sedi, nostro hoc votum roborante decreto: unde per sepe nominatum venerabilem Missum, Salomonem videlicet Constantie civitatis Episcopum, nobis hoc relatum est confirmandum ac postulatum est nostra auctoritate roborandum. Nos igitur subtili perpendentes examine animadvertimus propter instantem necessitatem & animarum lucra in gentibus demonstrata, utile fore. Omnia, quæ proficua Ecclesie probantur existere, & divinis non resultant preceptionibus licita & facienda esse non dubitavimus maxime in tam novelle Christianitatis plantatione , in qua varii eventus solent contingere. Quamobrem auctoritate omnipotentis Dei, & beatorum Apostolorum Petri et Pauli, & hoc nostro decreto, decrevimus secundum Reverendissimi Regis Ludovici votum, ipsas predictas dioeceses Hammaburgensem, Bremensem scilicet, & non deinceps duam sed unam esse & vocari, subdique sedi, que predecessoris nostri decreto Archiepiscopali est munere sublimata, restituta duntaxat de Bremensis Ecclesie rebus Episcopatui Werdensi parte inde ablata. Nullus vero Archiepiscopus Coloniensis ullam sibi deinceps in eadem dioecesi vindicet potestatem. Quinimo & ipsi & omnibus omnino suademus vere religionis cultoribus, ut sacra hac legatione fungentibus adjutorio & solatio sint, quatenus gratia hujus beneficii plenam mercedem recipere mereantur ab eo, qui dixit: Ite, docete omnes gentes, & quicunque receperit vos, me recipit. Itaque omnia a dilecto filio nostro Rege Ludovico ad hoc Deo dignum officium deputata, nostra etiam, pia ejus vota, auctoritate firmamus. Et quia casus præteritorum cautos nos faciunt in futurum, omnem quoque adversantem vel contradicentem atque nostris his studiis quolibet modo insidiantem, anathematis mucrone percutimus, atque perpetue ultionis reum diabolica sorte damnamus: ut culmen Apostolicum more prædecessorum nostrorum, causamque Dei pio affectu zelantes, ab adversis hinc inde partibus tutius muniamus. Et quia te, charissime fili Ansgari, divina clementia nova in sede primum disposuit esse Archiepiscopum, nosque pallium tibi, ad missarum solennia celebrandra, tribuimus, quod tibi in diebus tuis, uti & Ecclesiæ tuæ perpetuo statu manenti- bus privilegiis, uti largimur, Idcirco hujus indumenti honor morum vivacitate servandus est. Si ergo pastores ovium, sole geluque pro gregis sui custodia, ne qua ex eis aut errando pereat, aut ferinis lanienda morsibus rapiatur, oculis semper vigilantibus circumspectans, quanto sudore quantaque cura debeamus esse pervigiles nos, qui Pastores animarum dicimur, attendamus & ne susceptum officium in terrenis negotiis aliquanto implicare debeas admonemus. Vita itaque tua filiis tuis sit via, in ipsa, si qua tortitudo illis inest, dirigant: in ea, quod imitentur, adspiciant, in ipsa semper considerando, proficiant, ut tuum post Deum videatur bonum, quod vixerint. Cor ergo tuum neque prospera, que temporaliter blandiuntur, extollant, neque adversa dejiciant: districtum mali cognoscant, pium benevoli scatiant, insontem apud te inculpabilem malitia aliena non faciat, reum gratia non excuset, viduis ac pupillis injuste oppressis defensio tua subveniat. Ecce, frater charissime, inter multa alia ista sunt sacerdotii, ista sunt pallii, que si studiose servaveris, quod foris accepisse ostenderis, intus habebis. Veruntamen ista omnia superius annexa ab Apostolica sede Beatitudini tue indulta cognosce, si a fide & decretis sancte Catholice & Apostolice Romane Ecclesie in nullo penitus deviaveris. Quod si a fide & institutis aut sanctionibus te tanto sublimitatis honore sedis Apostolice declinare studiose presumseris, his nostris tibi collatis careas beneficiis. Porro te pallio uti, non nisi more sedis concedimus Apostolice, scilicet, ut successores tui, per semetipsos vel per Legatos suos & scriptum, fidem nobiscum tenere, ac sanctas sex Synodos recipere, atque decreta omnium Romane sedis Presulum, & epistolas, que sibi delata fuerint, venerabiliter observare atque perficere omnibus diebus suis scripto se & juramento profiteatur.

Scriptum per manum Zacharie Notarii Sancte Romane Ecclesie, in mense majo, indictione VI. Bene valete. Date pridie Calendas Junii per manum Tiberii Primicerii sancte sedis Apostolice.

Letter from bishop Ansgar to the prelates of King Louis I the Pious
(858 AD)

In the name of the holy and individual Trinity. Anscharius, Archbishop of the grace of God, to all the princes of the holy Church of God in the reign of King Louis. I want you to know, because it is contained in this book, how Ebbo, Archbishop of Reims, inspired by the divine Spirit, in the time of Lord Louis the Emperor, with the consent of him and of almost the whole of his kingdom gathered together in a Synod, went to Rome, and there received from the Venerable Pope Paschal a license to evangelize the public in the parts of the North. And how afterwards the emperor Louis exalted this work, and in all things, he provided liberally and benevolently, and the rest that happened to this Legation. For which reason I implore you to intercede with God, in so far as this Legation deserves to grow and bear fruit in the Lord. For the propitiation of Christ, and among the Danes and among the Swedes, the Church of Christ was founded, and the Priests, without prohibition they perform their own duty. I also pray that you will store these letters in your library for a perpetual memory, and as the place dictates, both you and your successors, where you see your usefulness, make this known to all. Almighty God make you all partakers of this pious benevolence and share in the heavenly glory of Christ.

In nomine sanctæ & individuæ Trinitatis. Anscharius gratia Dei Archiepiscopus omnibus sanctæ Dei Ecclesiæ Præsulibus in regno duntaxat Ludovici Regis commanentibus. Nosse vos cupio, quia in hoc libello continetur, qualiter Ebbo Remensis Archiepiscopus, divino afflatus Spiritu, temporibus Domini Ludovici Imperatoris, cum consensu ipsius ac pene totius regni ejus Synodi congregate, Romam adiit, ibique a Venerabili Papa Paschali publicam evangelizandi licentiam in partibus Aquilonis accepit. Et qualiter postea Ludovicus Imperator hoc opus sublimavit, seque in omnibus largum præbuit & benevolum, & cætera quæ huic Legationi contigerunt. Qual propter suppliciter deprecor, ut apud Deum intercedatis, quatenus hæc Legatio crescere & fructificare mereatur in Domino. Jam enim Christo propitio, & apud Danos & apud Sueones Christi fundata est Ecclesia, & Sacerdotes. absque prohibitione proprio funguntur officio. Precor etiam ut has literas in bibliotheca vestra ad perpetuam memoriam reponi faciatis, & prout locus dictaverit tam vos quam successores vestri, ubi utilitatem vestram perspexeritis, notum omnibus istud faciatis. Omnipotens Deus faciat vos omnes hujus operis pia benevolentia participes, & in cœlesti gloria Christi cohæredes.

If Shepherds of Sheep
(Dec. 1, 865)

Bishop Nicholas, servant of the servants of God, to our most reverend and most holy brother Rimbert, Archbishop of Hamburg.

If the shepherds of the sheep are content to bear the sun and frost for the protection of their flocks day and night, lest any of them perish either by wandering, or be snatched by the woolly bites of wild beasts, they watch over them with ever-watchful eyes; with how much sweat and with what care we must be vigilant, we who are called shepherds of souls, let us pay attention and not cease to present the duty we have undertaken towards the care of Sunday's sheep, lest in the judgment of the divine examination for our laziness before the supreme Shepherd the guilt of negligence may be excruciating. Wherefore, only by the reverence of honor are we judged more exalted among the rest. And we grant the mantle to your fraternity to celebrate the solemnities of the masses, which we give to you in no other way, with the privileges of your Church remaining in its state, except only on the day of the holy and venerable resurrection of our Lord Jesus Christ, or on the birthdays of the holy Apostles, and John the Baptist, and not only in the assumption of the blessed mother Mary, and at the same time on Sunday, the day of the birth of our Lord God, and equally on the day of the solemnity of your church, but also on the birthday day of your ordination we grant, as it was sanctioned by our most blessed predecessor, Lord Gregory, the presbyter of this soul. But your fraternity must put on a mantle in the Secretary, and thus go to the solemnities of the masses, and nothing more arrogate to itself by the boldness of reckless presumption, let alone by outward appearance anything be seized disorderly, even in order what might be allowed, be lost. We exhort you that the honor of your dress should be preserved by the vivacity of your modest actions, that the ornaments of your life should be in harmony with each other, in order that you may be seen by God as the author on both sides. that which they imitate, let them look at it, always considering themselves, and make progress, so that it may be seen that yours, after the Lord, is what they live in. The heart, then, should not be exalted by good fortunes that are temporarily flattered, nor be cast down by adversity, but whatever it may be, it should be conquered by the power of patience. Let hatred find no place with you, let no indiscriminate favor find, let them know the district of evil, let the foolish one be guilty with you, let no evil suggestion be made, the guilty, let him not excuse with grace, show not thy pardon to the transgressors, lest thou allow that which has not been avenged to be perpetrated. Let there be in thee the sweetness of the good shepherd, and let there be strict discipline of the judges, namely, one thing to encourage the innocent living, another to check the restless from perversity. But as sometimes the zeal of the superiors, while the district of the wicked wants the avenger to exist, has passed into the cruelty of reproof, restrain your anger with judgment, and censure follow discipline, that you may strike faults, and not depart from the love of the persons whom you correct. As virtue allows you to show mercy to the poor, let your defense help the oppressed, modestly contradict the oppressors with correction, look no one in the face against justice. The guard of equity excels in you, so that the rich may not by their power persuade you to listen to anything outside the way of reason, nor cause the poor to despair of their own affairs. How can you exist in mercy to God, such as the sacred reading prescribes, saying that a bishop must be blameless, but in all these things you can be healthy, if you have the charity of a teacher, which he who has followed does not at any time depart from what is right. Behold, dearest brother, among many other things these are the priesthood, these are the mantles, which if you diligently keep, what you show that you have received outside, you will have inside. And yours, which you wrote briefly within the epistles, although you had to explain it to the laity, we thank our Redeemer, because we knew that it was right in its very brevity. The Holy Trinity surrounds our fraternity with the protection of its grace, and so directs us in the way of its fear, that after the bitterness of this life we deserve to arrive together at the eternal sweetness.

Written by the hand of Zacharias Scriniarius of the holy Roman Church, in the month of December. Indiction 14.

Si pastores ovium

Nicolaus episcopus, servus servorum Dei, reverendissimo & sanctis- simo confratri nostro Rimberto Archiepiscopo Hammaburgensi.

Si pastores ovium solem geluque pro gregis custodia die ac nocte ferre contenti sunt, ut ne qua ex eis aut errando pereat, aut ferinis laniata morsibus rapiatur, oculis semper vigilantibus circumspectant; quanto sudore, quantaque cura debemus esse pervigiles, nos, qui pastores animarum dicimur, attendamus & susceptum officium exhibere erga custodiam dominicarum ovium non cessemus, ne in judicio divini examinis pro nostra desidia ante summum Pastorem negligentiæ reatus excruciet. Unde modo honoris reverentia sublimiores inter cæteros judicamur. Pallium autem tuæ fraternitati ad missarum solemnia celebranda concedimus, quod tibi non aliter, Ecclesiæ tuæ privilegiis in suo statu manentibus, uti largimur, nisi solummodo in die sanctæ ac vene randæ resurrectionis Domini nostri Jesu Christi, seu in natalitiis sanctorum Apostolorum, atque B. Baptiste Johannis, nec non in assumtione beatæ genetricis Mariæ, simulque in dominicæ Domini Dei nostri nativitatis die, pariterque in solemnitatis ecclesiæ tuæ die, verum etiam in ordinationis tuæ natalicio concedimus die, sicuti a beatissimo prædecessore nostro Domino Gregorio hujus almæ sedis præsule, sancitum est. In Secretario vero tua fraternitas pallium induere debeat, & ita ad missarum solemnia proficisci, & nihil sibi amplius ausu temerariæ præsumptionis arrogare, nedum exteriori habitu inordinate aliquid arripiatur, ordinate etiam, quæ licere poterant, amittantur. Cujus quam indumenti honos, modesta actuum vivacitate servandus est, hortamur, ut & vitæ ornamenta conveniant, quatinus auctore Deo recte utrobique posses esse conspicuus, itaque vita tua filiis tuis sit regula, in ipsa, si qua tortitudo illis injecta est, dirigant in ea, quod imitentur, aspiciant in ipsa se semper considerando proficiant, ut tuum, post Dominum, videatur esse, quo vixerint. Cor ergo neque prospera que temporaliter blandiuntur extollant, neque adversa dejiciant, sed quicquid illud fuerit, virtute patientiæ devincatur. Nullum apud te locum odia, nullum favor indiscretus inveniat, districtum mali cognoscant, insontem apud te culpabilem, suggestio mala non faciat, nocentem, gracia non excuset, remissum te delin- quentibus non ostendas, ne quod ultus non fuerit perpetrari permittas. Sit in te & boni pastoris dulcedo, sit & judicis severa districtio, unum scilicet, quod innocentes viventes foveat, aliud, quod inquietos feriendos a pravitate compescat. Sed quam nonnunquam præpositorum zelus dum districtus malorum vult vindex existere transiit in crudelitatem correptio, iram judicio refrena & censura disciplinæ secuturæ, ut & culpas ferias, & a dilectione personarum, quas corrigis, non exedas. Misericordiæ te, prout virtus patitur pauperibus exhibere, oppressis defensio tua subveniat, opprimentibus modeste correctio contradicat, nullius faciem contra justiciam aspicias. Custodia in te æquitatis excellat, ut nec divitem potentia sua aliquid apud vos extra viam suadeat rationis audire, nec pauperem de re sua faciat humilitas desperare. Quatinus Deo miserante talis possis existere, qualem sacra lectio præcipit dicens, oportet Episcopum irreprehensibilem esse, sed hiis omnibus, ut salubriter poteris, si magistrum caritatem habueris, quam qui secutus fuerit a recto aliquando non recedit. Ecce, frater charissime, inter multa alia ista sunt sacerdotii, ista sunt pallii, quæ si studiose servaveris, quod foris accepisse ostenderis, intus habebis. Eidem autem tuam, quam intus epistolis breviter ascripsisti, licet laicis explanare debueras, redemtori tamen nostro gratias agimus, quod eam in ipsa tam brevitate rectum esse cognovimus. Sancta Trinitas fraternitatem nostram gratiæ suæ protectione circum det, atque ita in timoris sui via nos dirigat, ut post vitæ hujus amaritudines ad æternam simul pervenire dulcedinem mereamur.

Scriptum per manum Zachariæ Scriniarii sanctæ Romanæ Ecclesiæ, in mense Decembri. Indibtione XIIII .

When Apostolic Dignity
(Nov. 1, 872)

Bishop Adrian, servant of God's servants, to the most blessed Rimbert, Archbishop of the Holy Church of Hamburg, an eternal blessing.

When Apostolic dignity, which is not only to found the Church, but also to sublimate those founded by other spiritual architects of the Churches, we have deemed it worthy, dearest brother, to incline our ear to your request and the vow of your kindness. We therefore grant you, as was granted by our predecessors Gregory and Nicholas, that is to say, that the nations of the Wimodians, the Norblings, the Danes, the Norwegians, the Swedes, or any of the northern nations, may be submitted to the yoke of faith by your preaching to the see of Hamburg with spiritual devotion, and to all your successors, to the same leave the seat to be possessed forever. We also appoint you as our legate throughout all the northern kingdoms, and to all the bishops of the above-mentioned nations present and further benefiting you, with the subjects of your people, and to all your successors at the seat of Hamburg to have the use of the mantle on the feasts and times named for you by our predecessor, that is to say, at Easter, at Pentecost, on the Nativity of the Lord, on the Assumption, on the Nativity, on the Purification of St. Mary, on the Nativity of the Apostles, on Sundays, and on all the celebrated festivals in your diocese, your head should also be adorned with a miter, you should carry a cross before you, besides you and the holy Church of Hamburg and we confirm to all your successors, by Apostolic authority, whatever your Churches have already been handed over by the Christians, or have been further delegated, in parishes, in estates, in all things movable and immovable, in bonds of both sexes, so that the said Church may perpetually possess the inviolable power. If any one, however, has attempted to go against the privilege of this authority of ours, and in any way has attempted to break it in part or in whole, of whatever power or dignity he may be, let him perish by eternal excommunication with Judas, the betrayer of the Lord, unless he repents and satisfies the Church of Hamburg. And the observer of this admonition and judgment of ours may have the blessing of Almighty God, of the blessed Apostles, and of us, who act as their vicars. May the Holy Trinity deign to preserve your fraternity unscathed at all times, and after the bitterness of this age, may it lead to eternal happiness.

Written by the hand of Gregory the Notary and Clerk of the Holy Palace, in the month of November, by Indictment V. Given by the hand of John the Chancellor of the Holy Roman Church, after the celebration of masses before the altar of the blessed Peter the Apostle.

Quum Apostolicæ

Adrianus Episcopus, servus servorum Dei, beatissimo Reymberto sanctæ Hammaburgensis Ecclesiæ Archiepiscopo æternam benedictionem.

Quum Apostolicæ dignitatis est, non solum Ecclesiam fundare, sed & ab aliis Ecclesiarum architectis spiritualibus fundatas sublimare, dignum duximus, frater Charissime, pro petitionis tuæ voto aures debitas benignitatis tuæ inclinare. Concedimus igitur tibi, sicut a prædecessoribus nostris Gregorio & Nicolao concessum est, scilicet ut gentes Wimodiorum, Norblingorum, Danorum, Norvenorum, Suenorum, vel quascunque Septentrionalium nationun jugo fidei prædicatione tua subdideris ad sedem Hammaburgensem spirituali devotione possideas, & omnibus successoribus tuis, ad eandem sedem perpetuo possidendas relinquas. Legatum quoque nostrum te per omnia Septentrionalia regna constituimus omnibusque supradictarum nationum episcopos præsentes & amplius profuturos, cum subjectis sibi plebibus tibi, & omnibus successoribus tuis ad sedem Hammaburgensem usum pallii habendum in festis & temporibus a prædecessore nostro tibi denominatis, scilicet in pasca, in pentecoste, in natali Domini, in assumptione, in nativitate, in purificatione sanctæ Mariæ, in natalitiis Apostolorum, in dominicis diebus, & in omnibus festis in diœcesi tua celebribus, ornari quoque caput tuum mitra, portare ante te crucem, præterea tibi & sanctæ Hammaburgensi Ecclesiæ & omnibus successoribus tuis, auctoritate Apostolica firmamus, quæcunque Ecclesiæ tuæ jam a Christicolis tradita sunt, vel amplius delegata fuerint, in parochiis, in prædiis, in omnibus rebus mobilibus & immobilibus, in mancipiis utriusque sexus, ut ea Ecclesia prædicta inviolabili potestate perpetuo possideat. Si quis autem, contra hujus nostræ auctoritatis privilegium ire temptaverit, & quoquo modo in parte vel toto in frangere nisus fuerit, cujuscunque potestatis vel dignitatis sit, æterna excommunicatione cum Juda traditore Domini pereat, nisi resipiscat, & Ecclesiæ Hammaburgensi satisfaciat. Observator autem hujus nostræ ammonitionis & jussionis habeat benedictionem omnipotentis Dei, beatorumque Apostolorum, & nostram, qui eorum fungimur vicariatione. Sancta Trinitas fraternitatem tuam omni tempore conservare dignetur incolumen, atque post hujus Seculi amaritudinem, ad perpètuam ducat beatitudinem.

Scriptum per manum Gregorii Notarii atque scriniarii sancti palatii, in mense Novembrio Indictione V. Data per manum Johannis Cancellarii sanctæ Romanæ Ecclesiæ, peractis missarum celebrationibus ante altare beati Petri Apostoli.

With a pious desire
(May 1, 891)

Bishop Stephen, servant of the servants of God, to the Most Reverend and most holy Adalgar, Archbishop of the Holy Church of Hamburg, and to my brother, and after you in the same Church forever.

Since the pious desire of the will and the praiseworthy intention of devotion is always to be aided by the Apostolic studies, care must be taken to ensure that those things which are lawfully conducted, and conform to the form of equity, are not capable of being disturbed by any refutation, but must continue according to the unbreakable law, under the authority of God, and for this reason the Apostolic having promulgated the sanctions, proper to each one, which is available to reason to possess, the right demands to be confirmed, and which you requested, that we should make the privilege of your Church, and having strengthened it with the Apostolic protection, we allow it to remain in its original form, and we confirm it by Apostolic law, to you and to your holy Church of Hamburg and to your successors to possess and hold the dignity and proper territory with all estates and parishes, and with all things movable and immovable, with slaves of both sexes, which in pious memory our predecessor Gregory granted to your predecessor Ansgar, whom he ordained archbishop in your church, having been established by law and Louis, your son, desired to have the Church, and determined the Imperial power. We decree, however, that you may have the power to ordain Bishops under your parish and diocese, so that they may remain under your power, and the dignity of your Church safe. But if anyone has attempted to go against the privilege of our authority, and how he has attempted to break it in part or in whole, let him be excommunicated from the body and life-giving blood of our Lord Jesus Christ and the access and agreement of the holy Church of God. And the observer of this admonition and judgment of ours may have the blessing of Almighty God and the blessed Apostles, and ours, who act as his vicar.

Written by the hand of John the Secretary of the Holy Roman Church. In the month of May. An indictment XI.

Cum piæ desiderium

Stephanus Episcopus, servus servorum Dei, Reverendissimo & sanctissimo Adalgario sanctæ Hammaburgensis Ecclesiæ Archiepiscopo & confratri meo, & post te in eadem Ecclesia in perpetuum.

Cum piæ desiderium voluntatis & laudandæ devotionis intentio Apostolicis sit semper studiis adjuvanda, cura est sollicitudinis adhibenda, ut ea , quæ legaliter geruntur, & æquitatis formæ conveniant, nulla valeant refragatione perturbari, sed irrefragabili jure, Deo auctore , debent permanere, & ob hoc Apostolicis promulgatis sanctionibus, propria unicuique, quæ rationi suppetunt possidenda, fas exigit confirmari, & quem postulasti, ut privilegium tuæ faceremus Ecclesiæ, & Apostolica tuitione roboravissemus, eandem in pristinum totum manere concedimus, & Apostolico jure firmamus, tibi tuæque sanctæ Hammaburgensis Ecclesiæ successoribusque tuis illam dignitatem, & fines proprios cum prædiis omnibus & parochiis, & omnibus rebus mobilibus & immobilibus, cum mancipiis utriusque sexus possidere & tenere, quum piæ memoria Gregorius antecessor noster, Ansgario antecessori tuo, quem Archiepiscopum ordinavit in Ecclesia tua, concessit, stabilito scilicet jure, & Ludowicus ejus filius tuam voluerunt habere Ecclesiam & Imperiali definierunt potestate. Decernimus autem, ut potestatem habeas ordinandi Episcopos infra tuam parochiam & diœcesin, ita tamen, ut sub tua, tuæque Ecclesiæ salva dignitate, ipsius maneant potestate. Si quis autem contra hujus nostræ auctoritatis privilegium ire temptaverit, & quomodo, in parte, vel in toto frangere nisus fuerit, sit excommunicatus a corpore & vivifico sanguine Domini nostri Jesu Christi & sanctæ Dei Ecclesiæ aditu & conventione separatus. Observator autem hujus nostræ admonitionis & jussionis habeat benedictionem omnipotentis Dei beatorumque Apostolorum, & nostram, qui eorundem fungimur vicariatione. Scriptum per manum Johannis Secretarii sanctæ Romanæ Ecclesiæ. In mense Mai. Indictione undecinra.

We judge your Holiness
(895 AD)

Formosus, bishop-servant of the servants of God, greetings and Apostolic blessing to the most reverend and most holy brother Adalgar, Archbishop of Hamburg.

It is determined that your holiness, as it had been commanded, hasten to the Apostolic See, in so far as the dispute which is being aired between you and Herman, the most reverend Archbishop of Agrippinae-Colonia, of the Church of Bremen, has come to an end. But as he insists through the vicars, and multiplies his complaints, we are not a little surprised why I will not show your presence, at least through the vicar's defender. In which it is given to suspect the highest, not to hate contention, who tries to subvert the equity of the judgment. In particular, when the most holy Archbishop of Mainz, to whom he had been enjoined by his brothers and neighboring bishops to inquire into the truth about this matter, he wrote to us to indicate that when the most reverend bishops came to Frankfurt, an inquiry was made very diligently about this same matter and all the diocesan bishops of the same Cologne bishop: Franco videlicet of Tungren, Vodebald of Traject, Wolselmus of Mimigardeverdense, Drogo of Minden, Egelmarus of Osnabrug, under the pretext of testifying, have testified that until you no Presul of the Church of Bremen has disdained the way of subjection to that of Cologne, but always your predecessors, who presided over the same Church of Bremen, from in the times of their Christianity, I sat down to have been subjects of the colonies.

True, since it is not expedient to frustrate the testimony of so many men, and to hasten the appointed time for coming, or to delay the delegation of the legate, it seemed inhuman to consider the complaint of so many times and the constant insistence of the legates as nothing. By this means, lest the Church of Cologne should lose justice, and thence, lest the Church of Hamburg, which had been instituted for the call of the gentiles, should fail, destitute of support; dispensationally, we have decided that, as long as the aforesaid church of Hamburg is expanded so far by the divine suffrage grace, that it is able to establish bishoprics, it has the already mentioned Church of Bremen as a support, and whenever it is necessary in great and necessary canonical affairs, not by any subjection, but by a feeling of fraternal charity, of Hamburg. The Archbishop of the Church, who holds the government of the same Church of Bremen by himself, or the Vicar, taking his turn, should be invited to go to the aide-de-camp of the Archbishop of Cologne. But the enlarged Church of Hamburg, supported by the benefactor of all goods, and founded by bishoprics, should receive the Church of Bremen, the seat of Cologne, so often mentioned. For it is inhumane among the seculars, to penetrate foreign laws, to transgress the boundaries established by the fathers of the most holy bishops, and to quarrel with those who ought to set examples of peace to their subjects. And this dispensation was decreed for this purpose, that peace may prevail, strife cease, and the rigor of justice be moderated by the compression of mercy. Knowing that without the good of peace, no service would be acceptable to God. Therefore, nor to people at all.

Apostolic Blessing
(Feb. 2, 905 AD)

Bishop Sergius, servant of God's servants, to the Most Reverend and most holy Adalgar, Archbishop of the Church of Hamburg.

Apostolic blessing and paternal consolation, receiving your fraternity's letters, knowing in them the insults of your Church and inflicted on you, not only about it, but about the iniquitous consent of Pope Formosa and Hermann of Cologne, and We are saddened by the unjust circumcision and judgment of the Archbishop of Mainz and other bishops. For what is more injurious than to deprive the churches of the honors justly handed over to them, and what is even more unjust? Than to violate and infringe upon the many privileges of the Apostles, handed down by the charters of Emperors and Kings, nothing more is granted by us or our successors, the words of the Lord, you are Peter, and upon this rock I will build my Church, and according to these words of the Apostles, you are built upon the foundation of the Apostles and Prophets in Christ Jesus himself as the cornerstone. It is agreed that the holy and universal Church was founded on Peter and the foundation of the Prophets and Apostles and compacted in the very cornerstone and firmest stone Christ Jesus, it is necessary that the same Stone and Apostolic foundation and the compaction of the holy cornerstone be firm, eternal and immovable, so that every Ecclesiastical superstructure should be stable and stable, and inviolable by all human presumption. We, therefore, in accordance with the Sunday and Apostolic voice, and in accordance with this opinion of the blessed Gregory, whatever has once been annulled by the privilege of the Church, must continue to be approved and established, whatever, therefore, by the iniquitous consent of Pope Formosus and Arnolf the king, and by the machination of Archbishop Herman in Thee and in the Church of Hamburg it was perpetrated recklessly, we also contradict and completely destroy it with our authority and the judgment of the majority of our brothers and under anathema. And whatever was granted to the Church of Hamburg by Pope Nicholas, and to our other predecessors, that is, to have archiepiscopal power over the kingdom of the Danes, the Norwegians, the Swedes, and all the Northern nations, and we decree and confirm that the Church of Bremen and the Church of Hamburg itself are not two, but one Church and parish. Therefore, by Apostolic authority and censure, under the protest of the divine judgment and the prohibition of anathema, we decree that no person of any order or dignity shall be those who either hold the Archbishopric dignity, or those who were granted by our predecessors to your Church and to you in the conjunction of the Churches of Bremen and Hamburg, and they were reformed by us, violet. But whosoever shall change, or presume to violate in anything, by the authority of God and of the blessed Peter the Apostle, and of us, who act as his vicar, shall be sacrificed to the bond of perpetual anathema. And Hermannus the Archbishop of Cologne, and Haddanus the Archbishop of Moguntine, for the satisfaction of penitence, we suspend from the divine office until the time appointed by us, since by them the privileges granted to your Church and your Apostolic See, and the Testaments of the glorious Emperors, have been annulled by them. We also, as you have prayed, have warned Wigbert and Bison, the Most Reverend Bishops and your neighbors, by letters, to the extent that they will help you and to ordain bishops suitable to you, in the places in which you can be found canonically, and the competent reason has been designated. Therefore, most holy Brother, your sanctity will be for us and for the universal Holy Roman Church, and we will be instructed how and where you will ordain bishops.

Dated by the hand of St. Peter the Chancellor, of the Roman Ecclesiae, on the fifth day of February, by Indiction III.

Arbitramur tuam sanctimoniam

Formosus Episcopus Servus servorum Dei, reverendissimo & sanctissimo fratri Adalgario Archiepiscopo Hamburgensi salutem & Apostolicam benedictionem.

Arbitramur tuam sanctimoniam, prout injunctum fuerat, ad Apostolicam sedem festinare, quatenus disceptatio, quæ inter te & Hermannum Agrippinæ Coloniæ reverendissimum Archiepiscopum ventilatur de Bremensi Ecclesiæ, finem perciperet. Sed eo per vicarios insistente, & quærimonias multiplicante, cur tuam non exhibuero præsentiam, saltem per defensorem Vicarium, non modicum miramur. In quo suspicari tribuitur summopere, contentionem non odire, qui judicii æquitatem conatur sub-terfugere. Præsertim cum & Moguntia sanctissimus Archiepiscopus, cui de hac re, ut veritatem inquireret, per confratres & conlimitaneos Episcopos, injunctum fuerat, ad nos scribens significaverit: quatenus venientibus reverendissimis Episcopis ad Frankenford, de hac eadem re diligentissime facta fuerit inquisitio omnesque diocesani ejusdem Coloniensis Episcopi: Franco videlicet Tungrensis, Vodebaldus Trajectensis, Wolselmus Mimigardeverdensis, Drugo Mindensis, Egelmarus Osnabrugensis, sub testificationis prætextu, testificati sunt, usque ad te nullum Bremensis Ecclesiæ Præsulem modum subjectionis Coloniensi antistiti contempsisse, sed semper prædecessores, tuos, qui eidem Bremensi Ecclesiæ præfuerunt, a temporibus suæ Christianitatis, sedi Coloniensi fuisse subjectos. Verum, quia tantorum virorum testimonium frustrari non expedit, & ad statutum veniendi tempus festinare, vel delegare legatum distulisti, tanti temporis querimoniam ac Legatorum constantem instantiam nihili perpendere inhumanum videbatur. Quapropter arctati, hinc ne Coloniensis Ecclesia justitiam perderet, inde, ne Hamburgensis Ecclesia quæ ad Gentium vocationem instituta fuerat subsidio destituta deficeret, dispensative censuimus, quatenus, quoad usque divina suffragante gratia præfata Hamburgensis Ecclesia in tantum dilatetur, ut Episcopia instituere valeat, jam memoratam Ecclesiam Bremensem in subsidium habeat, & quoties in magnis & prænecessariis canonicis negotiis oportuerit, non subjectione aliqua, sed affectu fraternæ charitatis, Hamburgensis Ecclesiæ Archiepiscopus, qui ejusdem Bremensis Ecclesiæ regimen obtinet per se, aut Vicarium, suàm vicem gerentem in adjutorium Coloniensis Archiepiscopi invitatus accedat. Dilatata autem Hamburgensi Ecclesia, largitore omnium bonorum adminiculante, &

fundatis Episcopiis, sæpe memorata Coloniæ'sedes Bremensem recipiat Ecclesiam. Inhumanum enim est inter seculares, aliena jura pervadere, quantomagis sanctissimorum Episcoporum statutos a patribus transgredi terminos, & eos litigare, qui pacis debent subditis exempla præbere. Hæc autem ad hoc decreta est dispensatio, ut pax vigeat, cesset contentio & justitiæ rigorem misericordiæ compressio temperet; scientes, sine pacis bono nullum Deo munus fore acceptabile. Nulli igitur omnino hominum.

Sergius Episcopus, servus servorum Dei, Reverendissimo & sanctissimo Adalgario Hammaburgensis Ecclesiæ Archiepiscopo, Apostolicam benedictionem & paternam consolationem, susceptis tuæ fraternitati literis cognitis in eis injuria Ecclesiæ tuæ & tibi illata, non solum de ea, sed de iniquo Formosi Pape consensu & Hermanni Coloniensis & Moguntini Archiepiscopi & aliorum Episcoporum iniqua circumventione & judicio, contristati sumus. Quid namque injuriosius quam privari ecclesias juste sibi traditas honoribus, quid etiam iniquius? Quam violare & infringere Imperatorum & Regum cartis tradita plurima Apostolorum privilegia, nil amplius a nobis vel successoribus nostris ratam, verba dominica, tu es Petrus & supra hanc petram ædificabo Ecclesiam meam, & juxta hæc verba Apostoli, estis superædificati super fundamentum Apostolorum & Prophetarum in ipso angulari lapide Christo Jesu. Constat sanctam & universalem Ecclesiam fundatam esse supra Petrum & fundamentum Prophetarum & Apostolorum, & compactum in ipso angulari & firmissimo lapide Christo Jesu, necesse est ut sic ipsa Petrea & Apostolica fundatio & sancta angularis compactione firma, æterna & immobilis, ita omnis Ecclesiastica superædificatio sit rata & stabilis, & ab omni humana præsumtione inviolabilis. Nos ergo juxta vocem Dominicam & Apostolicam, & juxta hanc B. Gregorii sententiam, quæcunque Ecclesiæ privilegio semel indulta fuerint, rata amplius & stabilita permanere debent, quicquid igitur iniquo consensu Formosi Papæ & Arnolphi Regis, & machinatione Hermanni Archiepiscopi in Te & in Ecclesiam Hammaburgensem temere perpetratum est, auctoritate quoque nostra & juditio plurimorum confratrum nostrorum & sub anathemate contradicimus & omnino destruimus. Quicquid autem a Nicolao Papa, & cæteris prædecessoribus nostris Hammaburgensi Ecclesiæ concessum est, scilicet habere Archiepiscopalem potestatem in regnum Danorum, Noruenorum, Sueuorum, & omnium Septentrionalium nationum & Bremensem Ecclesiam & ipsam Hamburgensem Ecclesiam non duas, sed unam esse Ecclesiam & parochiam decernimus & confirmamus. Auctoritate ergo Apostolica & sensura, sub divini juditii obtestatione & anathematis interdictu statuimus, ut nulla persona cujuscunque ordinis aut dignitatis sit, ea quæ vel in Archiepiscopali dignitate, vel quæ in conjunctionis Bremensis & Hammaburgensis Ecclesiæ a prædecessoribus nostris Ecclesiæ tuæ & tibi concessa sunt, & a nobis reformata sunt, violet. Quicunque autem mutaverit, vel in aliquo violare præsumserit, auctoritate Dei & beati Petri Apostoli & nostra, qui ejus fungimur vicariatione, perpetui anathematis vinculo immolatus. Hermannum autem Coloniensem Archiepiscopum, & Haddanum Moguntinum Archipræsulem pro satisfactione pœnitentiæ usque ad præfinitum a nobis tempus, a divino suspendimus officio, quoniam apud Triburiam per eos inique cassata sunt, concessa Ecclesiæ tuæ & tibi Apostolica sedis privilegia , & gloriosorum Imperatorum annullata sunt Testamenta. Nos quoque quemadmodum precatus es, monuimus literis Wigbertum & Bisonem, Reverendissimos & tuos convicinos Episcopos, quatenus te adjuvent & ad te convenientes ordinare Episcopos, in quibus Canonice inveneris locis & competens designaverit ratio. Tua ergo, sanctissime Frater, sanctimonia erit pro nobis & pro universali sancta Romana Ecclesia, & nobis remanda qualiter & ubi Episcopos ordinaveris. Datæ per manum Petri Cancellarii S, Romanæ Ecclesiæ quinto Nonas Fe- bruarii, Indictione III.

LETTERS FROM THE NORTH

The Scriptorium Project is the work of a small group of lay people of various apostolic churches who are interested in the preservation, transmission, and translation of the works of the early and medieval church. Our efforts are to make the works of the church fathers accessible to anyone who might have an interest in Christian antiquities and the theological, philosophical, and moral writings that have become the bedrock of Western Civilization.

To-date, our releases have pulled from the Greek, Syriac, Georgian, Latin, Celtic, Ethiopian, and Coptic traditions of Christianity, and have been pulled from sundry local traditions and languages.